MORE PRAISE FOR
THE LEADERSHIP TEST

"A high-impact experience. Simple, elegant, and profound. A short enough read to keep a busy exec's (or busy mom and dad's) attention, and meaningful enough to invoke personal inventory, reflection and action. I was reflecting on all my relationships at work and at home as I read the story."

Christopher Germann
Vice President, Executive Programs, Gartner, Inc.

"Clark does a brilliant job of bringing us back to basics and defining what drives authentic leadership. This book will be required reading for both aspiring and practicing leaders in my company."

Wesley Bull
President, Sentinel Training & Logistics, LLC

"*The Leadership Test* was refreshing and inspiring. Most books about leadership are sterile and hard to choke down, but this one was surprisingly different. After you read this book, you'll look at yourself differently and ask the hard questions about your influence and intent as a leader. I'm going to share this book with all of my friends."

Tiffany Watkins
Senior Administrator, Operation Kids

"This book took me on a powerful journey into the essence of leadership. It will be a wake-up call for many leaders and a handbook for those of us who are preparing to move into positions of leadership. I highly recommend it."

Benjamin Bloomfield
Graduate Student, University of Virginia

THE
LEADERSHIP
TEST

Will You Pass?

From the Author of *Epic Change*

Timothy R. Clark, Ph.D.

Library of Congress Control Number: 2009911780

ISBN: 978-0-578-04210-7

BUSINESS & ECONOMICS/Leadership
BISAC: BUS071000

Published by Oxonian Press
PO Box 1662
55 Merchant Street
American Fork, Utah, 84003

Printed in the United States of America

Book design and layout by Kelli Nilson

First Edition

www.theleadershiptest.com

To my children
and the next generation of leaders

CONTENTS

THE
LEADERSHIP
TEST

INTRODUCTION

What is the scarcest resource in the world? Ask any kindergarten teacher and the answer is attention. But there are other answers—oxygen to the scuba diver, mindshare to the blogger, cell phone minutes to the teenager, variety to the assembly-line worker. All good answers. But there's a better one. Leadership.

Its absence is the pandemic of our time. We don't need more smart people. We have plenty of those. It's a poverty of principle we face, a crisis of character.

Leadership is about stewardship, not self-interest. It's about moral responsibility for your life, other people, and the resources we share. Too often, this is not the pattern. What we see instead are leaders intoxicated with power, thirsting for adulation, vaunting themselves as if we were lucky to have them. And what do they leave? The littered remains of indulgence, greed, and corruption. How sad it is to leave a landfill when you could leave a legacy.

The universal temptation of leadership is to use position for personal gain. The culminating test of leadership is to resist that temptation. But as we all observe, many succumb. In far too many instances, leaders become lords of entitlement.

We see venal cartoon characters auctioned to the highest bidder. We see public figures clamor for praise and tribute from the less exalted. We see role models who don't model. We see image makers who would rather impress than bless. And yet we go on believing that leadership is about IQ points and the charismatic arts, as if they will save us. They never will.

The essence of leadership seems lost in the archives. Skills and experience matter. Of course they do. But the enduring truth remains that a leader's integrity is the true measure of greatness.

The story you are about to read is the story of a young man and his teacher. The teacher tutors the young man in the first lessons of leadership. Ultimately, the young man must take the test of leadership—a test that, sooner or later, thrusts itself on all of us.

Now the story.

CHAPTER

1

The Teacher

Isadore Kroll was a bookish little man. Every day, he dutifully appeared in his trademark ensemble—a bow tie and tennis shoes. But the culminating feature of his appearance was the hair. Either it wouldn't yield to the brush or the two had never met. Bushy, unkempt, undomesticated hair was his treasured affectation.

You see, even the most unpretentious human beings delight in at least one signature statement. It comes in handy if you need a little boost in your confidence. As a new teacher, Izzy, as they called him, needed such a boost when he first arrived.

Now, he was an institution, an urban oracle—at least to a few high school students in a tough section of Chicago.

He taught underprivileged, underachieving youth in an underfunded school in an underappreciated neighborhood, deep in the old city's industrial bowels—a combination that overwhelmed, overworked, and overcame the most well-intentioned.

Then a most unusual thing happened. Izzy ascended to the height of his powers. He rocked the literary world and won the Pulitzer Prize for a gracefully written account of Chicago's ethnic history. For the first time, writing's most coveted award went to a high school teacher, a distinction that has remained ever since.

As you can imagine, that singular event gave the hitherto unknown school a measure of self-respect and bestowed adoration on an unlikely hero. He could now draw a paying crowd. But he would not.

Izzy stayed. In spite of his instant celebrity and a flood of offers to move up in the world, he refused. He had received the highest of praise, and yet he carried on as if nothing had changed. Here he was—still eating school lunch, still grading essays about the meat-packing industry at the turn of the century, still doing the heavy lifting that wasn't always uplifting.

For a decade they called, and for a decade he turned them down. They would bring him into the fold. They would pay him a small fortune, furnish him with a cozy nest, set him up splendidly to live the life of the mind in the gilded salons of the literati. He could forget about the bleak and mundane things of the world.

The answer was always the same. "I like it here," he would say. They would nod in deference. Privately, they were offended and stupefied. It's one thing to be loyal, but this was a gritty inner city school. He'd done his time. It's noble to be committed to your calling, but what is there to be cherished about at-risk youth and overwhelming odds? Why would this celebrated man of letters stay when the success stories were so few and far between? What possessed him to grind away in this blighted spot?

This was the teacher.

CHAPTER
2
The Student

It was a long-standing tradition for Izzy to give his "Smart or Dumb" lecture on the first day of class. It was a sticky lecture. It stuck to the students. It stuck in their heads like the gum under their chairs.

"Take out a piece of paper," Izzy began, his instruction eliciting an audible murmur. "I want you to take notes. You're going to write down a few simple words."

Izzy went to the board and wrote in giant letters—Smart or Dumb.

He turned around. "Well," he scolded. "Write it down." Then he added a question mark, hitting the chalk board hard for emphasis as he placed the dot.

Smart or Dumb?

He rotated back to face the students. "Smart or dumb?" he asked rhetorically, underlining the words to match the cadence of his voice. "Are you smart or dumb?" he repeated in a high, nasal voice. The question sliced the air, halted the side-bar conversations, and silenced the adolescent bravado.

"People say the kids around here are disadvantaged." Izzy paused and then leaned into his next statement. "They're right," he said with disapproval. "Some of us are disadvantaged. We have a nasty little problem. We think we're dumb. As you will learn in this history class, subjugated people have a habit of taking on the language of their conquerors. Some of us have done that."

He walked slowly to the other side of the room. "How many of you have been told you're dumb?" he continued. All hands climbed slowly in unison. The teacher surveyed the damage and then replied, "It's tough to learn when you've been told this. It's impossible to learn when you believe it.

"If you fail in school, no one will be surprised," he declared. "How do you feel about that?" The shock value of his comment hushed the room.

Izzy spread his arms in a grand gesture. "Let's change the question. How many of you have the ability to learn?" All hands climbed quickly in unison. Izzy smiled. "This is interesting," he said. "So you all have the ability to learn." The suspense spiked as all eyes rested on the little man in front.

"I have to confess," the teacher continued. "I don't know what it means to be smart. I don't know what it means to be dumb. I don't think you know." He paused. "Who does know? A lot of people think they know, but the tools we use for measuring human intelligence are crude. Some people take it as their right to know. They ordain some as smart and banish others as dumb.

"I grew up in this neighborhood, you know. When I was a kid, they told me I was dumb. Then they changed their minds. Now they think I'm smart. It's a bit confusing, isn't it?" Izzy threw back his head and laughed to himself. "Society is often wrong. It gives a lot of wrong answers. It has given you the wrong answer. What are you going to do about that?"

The teacher paced back and forth and said nothing. Then he stopped. "Some of you need permission to explode the myth of your own dumbness. You have my permission," he said. "The only thing we know for sure is that we have the ability to learn, and that ability has no end."

Izzy went back to the board and ran his chalk through the words he had written. "Go ahead," he prodded, motioning with the chalk. The students applied twice the pressure to their pencils, scratching deep lines through the offending words.

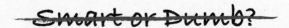

~~Smart or Dumb?~~

Izzy moved to the center of the room, held up his right hand, and with his index finger extended, proclaimed, "We have a rule in my class. We do not use the words *smart* or *dumb*. We do not use them because we do not know what they mean. We do not use them because they do more harm than good. We will unlearn these words. That won't be easy. To unlearn something is nearly always harder than to learn it in the first place. But we will. We will disabuse ourselves of any belief in these words.

"Outside of this classroom, you will start to see with new eyes. You will see the tyranny and calamity of the idea that some people are smart and others are dumb. You will see what a destructive fiction this really is."

Clearly exercised, Izzy paused to compose himself. Then he whispered as if he were revealing a little-known secret. "Your potential to learn and succeed in life is unknown and unknowable. You have no idea what you can learn and become, and nobody else has either.

There are no smart or dumb students at this school. They don't exist."

The students sat wide-eyed.

"Here's the next word I want you to write down." Izzy went to the board and in giant strokes wrote:

Confidence

"Let me teach you a principle," he said. "Learning requires confidence. In fact, you can't have one without the other. They are friends. They travel together. They can't be separated. You can't learn without confidence nearby. You will only learn as your confidence allows you to learn. Without confidence, you won't even try."

Some of the students started fidgeting nervously.

"Here's a trick question. How do you learn if you don't have the confidence to learn?" The room fell silent. Finally, a young man broke the tension.

"Yes, Sir?" inquired Izzy.

"You just have to try," the student said with trepidation.

Izzy scanned the room. "Did everyone hear that?" he asked.

"Young man, what's your name?"

"Marcus," responded the boy.

"Marcus, please come up here and repeat what you said to the entire class and then I want you to write your answer on the board."

Marcus thought about declining the offer, but knew it was too late. He walked haltingly to the chalk board and wrote:

Just Try

Once the young man got back to his chair, Izzy turned to the class. "What just happened?" he inquired.

A young woman on the front row raised her hand.

"Please," Izzy said, motioning her to reply.

"He did that."

"He did what?"

"He just tried."

Izzy nodded approvingly, bringing the discussion to a climax. "Marcus," he said, "how much confidence do you have now?"

Marcus smiled, "A little more."

"A lot more or a drop more?"

"A drop more," Marcus replied.

Izzy turned to the class. "That's how it works!"

"Here's my job," he said. "I will give you opportunities to learn. If you just try, that effort will drip-feed your confidence and your learning, and they will grow together. I can promise you one thing: If you try, you will see a transformation in yourself. You will look in the mirror and like what you see."

Marcus sat motionless in his chair. Here was a young man who had been mugged by society, labeled and assigned to the dumb category at a very early age. And like many kids assigned to the dumb category, he had accepted the verdict because, for the most part, children believe what they are taught.

At this moment, however, this particular young man was not feeling submissive to his socialization. A storm was breaking loose in his head.

This was the student.

CHAPTER

3

The Question

Every hour the bell would release a flood of chatter into the halls. The high tide of commotion lasted ten minutes and then gradually receded as the students found their next classes. At three o'clock, the final wave would break and then quickly spill out of the building.

Izzy always joined the last wave. The eccentric gentleman would move from hall to hall, face to face, and hand to hand. He could press the flesh as deftly as any politician. But it wasn't votes he was after, just eye contact. And it wasn't favors he was trading, just affirmations. If you entered his line of sight, you were sure to come away with a little more confidence to try harder.

When the locker doors stopped banging and the last student was gone, Izzy shuffled down the silent hall and retired to his classroom before catching the bus home. It was a scene that repeated itself every working day.

One particular afternoon, the phone rang as the diminutive teacher settled into his chair.

He picked up the receiver. "Izzy Kroll," he said.

"Izzy. It's Marcus."

The storm that had broken loose in the young man's head seven years earlier had not abated. He had gone on to college, earned a degree in computer science, and taken a very fine job as a programmer with a software company in the suburbs.

"Marcus, how are you doing, my friend? It's been a while. How's the crackerjack programmer?"

Despite having taught thousands of students in a career that stretched more than two decades, Izzy didn't forget names or faces. His recall of personal facts was legendary, which he could use as ammunition to launch a barrage of questions at any time.

"Marcus, how's the software business? What projects are you working on? What's the latest stock tip?"

"Izzy, you shouldn't joke about things like that. Plus, you never know. They may be monitoring our call for customer service."

They both roared with delight.

Marcus got to the point. "Izzy, they want to promote me."

"Congratulations, Marcus. I knew sooner or later they would pull out Excalibur and tap you on the shoulder."

"No, it's not like that. My boss just got fired and they want me to be the new team leader."

"Do you want the job?" Izzy asked.

"I think so, but I've never been a boss."

"And chances are you'll never go back to programming if you take the job. Have you thought about that?"

"It makes me nervous."

"Good. It should. If you take the job, you will feel homeless for awhile."

"That's comforting."

"Marcus, it's normal. You will shift from working mostly with machines to working mostly with people. People behave very differently than machines."

"That's what I'm afraid of," said Marcus. "I don't know anything about leadership."

"Oh, yes you do. You're in a leadership role right now."

"Izzy, I'm just a programmer. I just do my job. No one reports to me. I'm not in charge."

Then came the tart reply. "Marcus, I could say the same thing—I'm just a teacher. I just do my job. No one reports to me. I'm not in charge."

"Marcus," the teacher explained, "You're a leader right now, in your current role. You're in charge of leading yourself. Do you have any idea how magnificent it would be if people could lead themselves? Self-directed leadership is the basis of all leadership."

"Makes sense, but here's my dilemma. I don't know where to start. Listen to this. I did a search online and found more than 375,000 books on leadership. Izzy, I need some help."

"Certainly. What's your question?"

"Where do I start?"

"That's easy. Start reading."

"Very funny, Izzy."

"Marcus, why are there so many books on leadership?"

"I don't know."

"Marcus, think. There are reasons."

"Because it's important?"

"Yes, keep going."

"Well, leadership is complicated."

"Think about it this way. If your search yielded that many titles, and we assume that the average width of a book spine is one inch, the stack of books on leadership would be over 30,000 feet high. That's higher than Mount Everest. Think harder. Why all the fuss?"

"Uh," Marcus hesitated. "Leadership is extremely important."

Izzy thought for a moment. "Would there be good music in a world without leadership?"

"What does music have to do with it?"

"Just answer the question," pressed Izzy.

"Probably not."

"Marcus, our high school band teacher was sick last week and we had no substitute, so our principal told the students to rehearse on their own. Even by a charitable definition, the sounds coming from the band room would not qualify as music.

"What about books? Would there be good books in a world without leadership?"

"I doubt it."

"You don't have to doubt," Izzy said. "The only books we would have would be trashy beach reads."

"Third question: What kind of restaurants would there be without leadership?"

"The high school cafeteria comes to mind."

"Last question: What kind of football teams would there be without leadership?"

"Now don't make fun of my Bears, Izzy. They'll be back."

"Maybe. That will depend on . . . ." Izzy waited for Marcus to finish the sentence.

"You're right. No leadership, no championship. I get it."

"You see. We have our answer. Without leadership, there would be no good music, no good books, no good restaurants, and no good football teams. There would be no reason to live! So why the mountainous literature on leadership?"

Before Marcus could respond, Izzy jumped in. "Let me say it a different way. With leadership, we get crescendos, heroes, culinary delights, and touchdowns. Leadership is the animating force that moves us forward. It brings meaning to our lives, in spite of our challenges." Then he paused. "There's just one small problem."

"What's that?" asked Marcus.

"Leaders are going extinct."

Izzy gazed out the window. For a brief moment he reflected on his life's work—to interpret and impart the sweep of history to his students.

"Marcus, leadership has no home. It belongs to none of the disciplines and none of the professions. Everybody's trying to figure it out. Everybody's looking for the secret."

Marcus leaned back in his chair and was seriously questioning whether he should have called his esteemed mentor. It was all beginning to sound too theoretical. After all, he was dealing with a real problem in the real world, and it seemed the conversation had drifted from the practical to the philosophical.

"They say that leadership is the one subject most written about and least understood," Izzy continued.

"That's starting to become pretty clear," offered Marcus.

The teacher opened a new line of questioning, "And why do you think that is?" he probed.

Marcus was now answering more out of respect than interest. "I would say it's because leadership is hard."

With the conversation reaching diminishing returns, Marcus began checking his e-mail.

"Leadership is not a mysterious art. It's simple in principle but hard in practice."

Marcus grew alert. "What did you just say?"

"I said leadership is not a mysterious art. It's simple in principle but hard in practice."

"Well that doesn't make sense, Izzy. How do you explain Mt. Everest."

"That's the deception of it all. The number of books reflects both the importance of the subject and the confusion around it. But it's really not that complicated."

"Izzy, if it's not that complicated, would you be so kind as to direct me to the right book. Then I won't have to worry about climbing Mt. Everest."

Izzy chuckled. "I hate to disappoint you, Marcus. I haven't found that book. Unless God wrote it and we can't find it, the much sought after grand theory of leadership has yet to be discovered."

Exasperated, Marcus responded, "If it's so simple in principle, it's got to be written down somewhere. Izzy, I'm under the gun. I owe the company an answer by next week."

The sage went silent for a moment. "Marcus, come over to the school and let's talk about it. How about lunch on Monday?"

Marcus reluctantly agreed. "Yeah, I can make it."

"Perfect. You know where to find me."

"I'll be there."

"Marcus?"

"Yes, Sir."

"One more thing: I've got some homework for you. I want you to think about this. The first question you need to ask yourself is not a *how* question, but a *why* question: *Why* do you want to lead?"

"You got that?" asked Izzy.

"Sure, but—"

"See you on Monday."

This was the question.

CHAPTER

4

The Answer

It had become a long-standing tradition for Izzy's former students to drop by the school for lunch. He never asked them to come. They just came.

But there was one rule, one command performance. When they came, they had to spend half the lunch hour talking to students. Izzy wanted them to mentor their younger counterparts.

"I don't want kids to *stay* in school," Izzy would say, shaking his hands in the air. "Who wants to *stay* in school? It makes you want to run. Who came up with such a brilliant slogan?" Unable to detect the irony in his own life, he would ask, "Since when did the word *stay* have motivational qualities? I want students to *come alive* in school."

Halfway through the lunch hour, Marcus got up to do his rounds. Anxious to talk to his mentor, he moved hastily from table to table, striking up hurried and awkward conversations—a fact not lost on the students. By the time the lunch bell rang, he had met his quota.

Marcus caught up with Izzy and the two of them walked back to the classroom. It was Izzy's free period.

Teacher and student sat down against the window. Pensive, Marcus positioned himself on the edge of the chair. "Izzy, I've thought about it all weekend. I'm going to take the job. It would be crazy not to. Can you just boil the leadership stuff down for me?"

Izzy laughed heartily. "You Millennials have no patience. Everything's on demand. Let me see what I can do to create a little frustration. Marcus, I know you're excited to jump into the saddle, but you didn't do your homework."

Izzy got up from his chair, grabbed a blank piece of paper from his desk and gave it to his former pupil.

"The first question of leadership has nothing to do with *how*. The first question is a *why* question. *Why* do you want to lead?"

Marcus started writing.

The first question of leadership is a <u>why</u> question: <u>Why</u> do you want to lead?

"Marcus, some people want to be president simply because they want to be president. That's not good enough. So let me ask you: Why do you want this job?"

"Izzy, what do you mean? Isn't that obvious?"

"No, actually it's not." Pressing him further, "Tell me why you want the job."

"It's a chance to move up. I'll earn more money. There's more visibility—you know, all of that. It's a no-brainer except for one thing."

37

"What's that?"

"I could fail and get fired like my boss."

Izzy took a deep breath and gathered his thoughts. "Marcus," he said, "Have you accepted the offer yet?"

"No. Not yet. I'm planning to this week."

"Good," Izzy said. "Let's go back to the *why* question. Think back on our history class. One of the most important things I taught you was how to recognize patterns. Remember? Good students see patterns. Poor students see chaos."

"I remember."

"I just noticed a pattern in your response to my question."

"What do you mean?"

"Whom did you talk about?"

"You asked me why I wanted the job."

"Exactly, and what did you say?"

"I gave you the reasons."

"Yes, and whom did you talk about?"

"Me."

"That's right. You talked about yourself. You talked only about yourself. Every part of your response was about you. Any pattern there?"

Feeling a little embarrassed, Marcus sat back in his chair.

"Did I chill your ambition?" asked Izzy.

"Just a little, thanks."

"Marcus, leadership is not about you." Izzy pointed to the window. "It's about them."

"Let me give you the definition of leadership. Are you ready?"

"Sure, go ahead."

"Leadership is the process of influencing volunteers to accomplish good things."

Marcus wrote it down.

Leadership is the process of influencing volunteers to accomplish good things.

"Influencing volunteers? What's that all about?"

"Leadership is the business of influence, but what kind of influence? That's the question. Think about it on a spectrum." Izzy spread his hands apart. "At one end of the spectrum is manipulation. At the other end is coercion. In the middle is persuasion. This is the spectrum of influence. Got that?"

The Spectrum of Influence

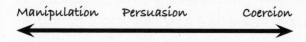

"So where is leadership?" Izzy inquired.

"Sounds like it's in the middle," answered Marcus.

"Exactly. All three may be considered forms of influence, but only persuasion is leadership. Only persuasion really helps people. The other two hurt people. Manipulation exploits. Coercion controls. Both can produce results, but not the best results, and not lasting results, and more often than not, very bad results.

"Marcus, remember our study of political systems?"

"Sure. That was my favorite part of the class."

"As we learned, most political systems in the world are endemically corrupt. That means corruption has spread throughout the system like cancer. Remember these?" Izzy rattled off the terms:

- Bribery
- Extortion
- Cronyism
- Patronage
- Graft
- Embezzlement
- Kickbacks
- Unholy Alliances

"I remember."

"Do you notice any relationship between the major forms of corruption and the spectrum of influence? Let's do a pop quiz. Now keep in mind, we may be in Chicago, but you only get one vote. What category of influence does bribery come from?"

"That would be manipulation."

"That's right."

"And kickbacks?"

"Same thing."

"How about extortion?"

"That would be in the coercion category."

"You get the picture. These are all tools of manipulation and coercion. Unfortunately, many societies depend on these tools to function. Now scale down to a smaller unit of analysis. Think about the family. What happens when a family operates on the basis of manipulation and coercion?"

"It's not good. Families break down, marriages fall apart, and children often repeat the same patterns."

"You understand the principle. Leadership is about influence-through-persuasion. If you cross over into manipulation or coercion, you leave leadership behind."

"Why do you use the word volunteers?" asked Marcus. "Why don't you just say people?"

"To further emphasize the distinction between influence and its neighbors to the east and west. When we acknowledge people as volunteers, we remind ourselves of the business we're in. As I said, leadership is the influence-through-persuasion business. Those we lead can choose to be led or not. They can choose to follow or not. They have the power to grant or withhold support, and we have the power to influence. No persuasion, no leadership."

Marcus looked puzzled. "What if you try persuasion and it doesn't work? What if people blow you off? Don't you have to bring the hammer down?"

"I'm not done, Marcus. Leadership has a front end and a back end. Persuasion is the front end. Accountability is the back end. Don't confuse the two. Persuasion includes all legitimate forms of influence, such as creating a vision, setting goals, using logic, data, and creativity, and demonstrating interest and concern for people. Not least is the power of your personal example. These are your tools. But here's the catch—if you lead through persuasion and fail to hold people accountable, you're just a fun guy to be around. You're not a leader.

"Here's the other point of confusion. Don't mistake accountability for coercion. Sometimes we see heavy-handed leaders who throw their weight around and we call it accountability. We get so backwards in our thinking that we praise autocrats and thugs for raw power, unbridled ambition, and extravagant glorification. We even call them strongmen as a compliment. Coercion isn't strength. It's just a poor substitute for good leadership.

"Accountability means you set clear and fair expectations, as well as clear and fair consequences for meeting or not meeting those expectations. You work with people in an open, honest, and respectful way with no surprises.

"Marcus, didn't you play football for both Coach Dewey and Coach Cordova when you were here?"

"Yeah, both of them."

"Any difference in approach between the two?"

Marcus rolled his eyes. "Coach Dewey was a screamer. Lots of drama. He was out of control, and everyone was scared of him."

"How was the accountability?" Izzy asked.

"To use your term, very little back end. We were really disorganized. Not a lot of follow through. We only won two games."

"How about Coach Cordova?"

"Way different. Things really changed when he came on board. If you messed up on a play, he pulled you. It was automatic. He didn't yell. He didn't say anything." Marcus paused for a moment. "You know, that's interesting. He had a good front end of persuasion and a good back end of accountability."

"What was your record under coach Cordova?"

"Ten and two."

"There you go. Marcus, look at all of the leaders out there. Most don't put persuasion and accountability together."

Marcus stared into the distance, reflecting on the new insight Izzy had shared.

"Make a note of this, Marcus. Leadership is based on influence-through-persuasion at the front end, combined with accountability at the back end."

Leadership is based on influence-through-persuasion at the front end, combined with accountability at the back end.

"It's interesting you say that, Izzy. This past year, our team at work has been late and over budget on its commitments, so our boss got more demanding. He started making threats and promises at the same time. He shifted to manipulation and coercion. He called me in one day and told me that if I could meet a certain deadline, I'd get a raise, but if I couldn't, I'd get fired."

"Wow, a fun guy and a mean guy combined. So what did you do?"

"Well, I'm the new kid on the team, so I worked my tail off to get the work done."

"Did you make the deadline?"

48

"Barely."

"Did you get the raise?"

"No. He didn't really mean it."

"How do you like that kind of leadership?"

"It stinks," Marcus said. "Speaking of patterns, I've noticed something interesting. When bosses try to show their big teeth, people respond in predictable ways. Poor performers are scared to death. They know they are at risk. Mediocre performers put their heads down and comply, but under the surface, they get passive-aggressive and stop caring."

"What about high performers?" Izzy asked.

"That's the most interesting part. High performers just laugh. They don't put up with it. And if the boss persists, they just leave because they have other options. That's why our two best programmers walked."

"And then they fired your boss?"

"That's right."

"So high performers aren't impressed with rank, I take it?"

"Not at all. It doesn't matter how many stripes you have on your shoulder. They're not wowed by that."

"It goes further than not being wowed, Marcus. When they laugh, it's their way of rejecting the leader and the leadership being offered. They are saying, 'No thank you. We do not accept you as our leader. We have disqualified you.' It's actually a pretty strong indictment."

"I never thought of it quite that way, but I think you're right. They really are saying 'thanks, but no thanks,'" replied Marcus.

"Tell me about your boss's intent," asked Izzy. "What was he trying to accomplish?"

"The normal things. Deliver quality, on time, and on budget."

"That's it?"

"Yeah, why?"

"Did he have any goals for the members of the team?"

"What do you mean?" Marcus asked.

"Well, you had performance goals. What about people goals?"

Marcus didn't answer.

"You're drawing a blank. Do you see anything wrong with that, Marcus?"

"I think I see the point. You need both kinds of goals."

"Marcus, leadership is about influence-through-persuasion combined with accountability.

But it's also about the intent to help people accomplish good things. Our intent is reflected in what we do and how we do it. Humans are pretty good at sniffing out intent. If your boss wasn't interested in your personal growth and development, what happens to his ability to influence you?"

"I get the picture."

"Write this down, Marcus. Leaders qualify themselves based on the manner of their influence and the nature of their intent."

Leaders qualify themselves based on the manner of their influence and the nature of their intent.

"Let's go back to our history class. We talked about two kinds of leaders. Do you remember?"

"Real leaders and fake leaders."

"I taught you well, Marcus," the teacher said with pride. "So it's really quite simple. Real leaders qualify as leaders based on, first, persuasion and accountability, and, second, the intent to accomplish good things. Fake leaders are in a different business—the manipulation and coercion business."

"Izzy, I still remember a picture you showed us in class of one of the fake leaders. He was some head of state somewhere and it was his funeral. He was lying in a casket in full dress uniform, covered in medals, ribbons, sashes, and swords. What got me was the line of ragged, hungry people waiting to pay their last respects."

"He wasn't in the leadership business was he? In fact, if you look at most leaders of nations throughout history, the pattern is to live large and let the people starve."

"I can see that," said Marcus.

"If you look at patterns of influence and intent, it's pretty easy to pick out the real leaders from the fake ones." Izzy returned to his earlier question. "When I asked you why you wanted to lead, what good things did you mention? What was your intent?"

Marcus winced, "Money, recognition, opportunity."

"Are these good things?" Izzy asked.

"I guess not," Marcus yielded.

"Hang on. Are you sure?"

"Well, they're good things for me."

"They are. Having good things in mind for yourself is good, but it doesn't make you a leader. That's why you have to start with the *why* question. Why do you want to get in the game? If it's to enrich yourself, you're in trouble right from the start, and so are the unfortunate people who come under your charge. I want you to think about two words. The first word is stewardship. The second word is self-interest. Self-interest needs no explanation, but the concept of stewardship deserves some attention. What is stewardship?" asked Izzy.

"Something you're in charge of, something you're trusted with?" Marcus offered.

"Close. Let's define it a little more clearly."

"Stewardship is moral responsibility for your life, others, and the resources we share."

Marcus scribbled furiously.

Stewardship is moral responsibility for your life, others, and the resources we share.

"In an organization, your stewardship begins with yourself and then extends to the welfare and interests of the organization, the people you lead, and even beyond. Here's the question: What do you do when there's a conflict between stewardship and self-interest, when you can't do both, when doing one comes at the expense of doing the other? What are you going to do then?"

Izzy continued, "Think about the reasons you want the job. What do you think everybody else wants?"

"The same things I want, more or less."

"That's right. You're no different from them. If you take the job, does it make you a little more special?"

"Of course not," answered Marcus.

"Back to my question then: What is the relationship between stewardship and self-interest?"

"Man, Izzy, you're not making this easy, are you?"

"No, I'm suspending influence! You have to answer the question."

Marcus responded, "I surrender. Stewardship comes first."

"Thank you. Now I realize that was a forced confession, so it doesn't count. The real question is whether you believe it. Do you?"

"Makes sense."

"Marcus, you may accept the logic, but do you believe it?"

"I think I believe it."

"Marcus, you're untested. If you take the job, that will change. Leadership is a proving ground. It will put pressure on your beliefs about stewardship and self-interest and the relationship between the two. The question will be whether you consistently put stewardship first.

"Sadly, most leaders succumb to the temptation to serve themselves. Just watch the news. There's a new float in the scandal parade almost every day. Marcus, most of human history is the story of non-leaders who squandered a chance to make a difference in the world. If you want someone to put self-interest above stewardship, just grab somebody off the street. Anybody can do that. But if you want a real leader, that's a different story. Those people are hard to find.

"There's no calling in life that is so frequently violated as the calling of leadership. And there is no greater disservice to our understanding of it than our indiscriminate use of the word. As I said before, we call anyone in a position of authority a leader, as if the position they occupy anoints them such. The two concepts have little to do with each other. Conferral of authority no more makes a leader than a blank canvas makes a painter, a baton makes a conductor, or a pen makes a writer.

"There's another thing," said Izzy. "We tend to think that leadership is about proportions.

Unless you have some big, important job, unless you deal with high profile issues, we don't call you a leader. Leadership is not defined by scale or scope. Small problems and opportunities are important too. Think about your own life. Think about taking this job. How important is this to you?"

"It's huge."

Izzy gave a confirming nod.

"Marcus, it's about time for the next class to start. You've got some more homework. Let me give you one more point to ponder: Leadership puts pressure on the relationship between stewardship and self-interest."

Leadership puts pressure on the relationship between stewardship and self-interest.

"If you take the job, you'll get a new title, a new position, more authority, and more money. But that won't make you a leader."

"I think you made that point pretty clear."

"I suppose I did," Izzy laughed. "But you still have a test to take."

"What's the test?" Marcus asked.

"I'm going to hold you in suspense—to be continued, as they say."

"Izzy, that's not fair."

"It's eminently fair, Marcus. You have homework. Wrestle these issues to the carpet. Push back. Challenge me. Do you agree or disagree, and what are you going to do about it?"

Marcus started to get up.

"Before you go, let's review your notes."

Notes

1. The first question of leadership is a *why* question: *Why* do you want to lead?

2. Leadership is the process of influencing volunteers to accomplish good things.

3. The spectrum of influence includes manipulation, persuasion, and coercion. Leadership is based on influence-through-persuasion at the front end, combined with accountability at the back end.

4. Leaders qualify themselves based on the manner of their influence and the nature of their intent.

5. Stewardship is moral responsibility for your life, others, and the resources we share.

6. Leadership puts pressure on the relationship between stewardship and self-interest.

This was the answer.

CHAPTER

5

The Test

The telephone rang.

"Izzy, it's Marcus."

"Marcus, what did you decide?"

"I'm wrestling and I'm not winning. Once I started thinking about my stewardship, it changed the analysis. Do you have a few minutes if I come by after school today?"

"Yes, come over. I'll see you in my office at four o'clock."

"See you then."

Marcus appeared in the doorway at the appointed hour.

"Come in, Marcus."

"Izzy, thanks for being so generous with your time. I'm having real doubts about accepting the offer. I like my job, and I don't know if I should give it up."

"You're doing the risk/reward calculation in your head, aren't you?"

"Exactly."

"Izzy, I want the job because . . . . You know what I mean. But it might not be worth the trouble. I can tell you what you want to hear. I can tell you that I want to help the organization and my team and make a contribution, but that's your answer. I'm not sure it's my answer."

"I like what I hear," replied Izzy.

Marcus looked puzzled.

"You've been wrestling with the *why* question. Doing a little soul-searching. Good. Let me complicate things a little more. Would you like to hear about the leadership test that you'll have to take?"

"I would."

"Marcus, when we talked last time, I told you that leadership is not a mysterious art, and I shared a few simple principles. But here's the thing you need to understand—leadership is an applied field. You can study it, think about it, and talk about it only so much. It doesn't really matter how much you know. Leadership is about doing.

"Once you step out there and start leading others, you're going to be tested. Every leader in the world has to take the test, and there's no cheating. The pass/fail ratio is not good. It goes back to what I shared with you about stewardship and self-interest. Remember? Leadership puts pressure on the relationship between stewardship and self-interest."

"I'm feeling that right now and I haven't even taken the job."

Izzy smiled. "You will be tested in different ways to see if you can keep stewardship above self-interest."

"Makes sense."

"It's not a one-time test either. You will be tested over and over because you want certain things and your stewardship requires certain things. There's natural tension there."

"I believe you."

"Rewards are good, Marcus. Earn them. But if you put your self-interest first, sooner or later, you'll let people down. That's what fake leaders do. Real leaders do the opposite.

"Did you bring your notes from our last visit?"

"I've got them right here." Marcus unfolded the wrinkled paper.

"Write this down. Putting stewardship above self-interest is an act of leadership."

Marcus turned over the paper and wrote.

Putting stewardship above self-interest is an act of leadership.

"You need to know this in advance. There will be times when the pressure on the relationship between stewardship and self-interest is intense. You need to be ready."

"Izzy, tell me what the test looks like."

"There are actually five tests rolled up into one. Whenever there's a conflict between stewardship and self-interest, there's a test."

Marcus sat up in his chair.

"The first one is the test of responsibility."

"How does it work?" asked Marcus.

"Your response on the first test will be a determining factor in every aspect of your life. This is where you set or extend your limits and capacity to lead."

Izzy continued. "Think of everyone walking around with packs on their backs. In our packs, we carry our responsibilities. Some people are eager to contribute and willing to do more. They square up under the load. Other people go around trying to empty their packs. I'm not suggesting that you pick up whatever people want to unload. People and organizations can make unreasonable and improper demands. Obviously, you have to use judgment. The test is whether you're willing to add more responsibility to your pack and do some of the heavy lifting.

"Marcus, what percentage of the population do you think is willing to do the heavy lifting?"

"Oh, I'd say less than half."

"It's true. If you're willing to carry a heavier pack, you immediately set yourself apart.

"Marcus, why do they want to promote you?"

"I guess because I've performed well."

"That's right. Organizations promote people into formal leadership based on their performance as individual contributors. You've given people clues about your ability to lead at the next level. In fact, you may have already passed the first test. Here's a way to find out. Do you turn down new assignments?"

"No. I figure it's part of my job to do what they ask me to do."

"Do you volunteer to take on new assignments?"

"I volunteered to be on the new product development team last year. And I've volunteered to help with a few other projects."

"You see? You've been willing to fill your pack. That's the first test."

The First Test: Fill Your Pack.

"When you fill your pack, you show a pattern of placing stewardship above self-interest. Think about your team. Does everyone on your team do this? Are they willing to fill their packs?"

Marcus laughed. "We seem to have three groups on our team. First, there's the 'how-can-I-help' group. They have a can-do attitude and are always willing to carry a heavier pack. Then there's the 'do-your-job-and-go-home' group. They work 'till five and say good bye. They're good soldiers, but they refuse to cross the line and step out of their comfort zones. Finally, there's the 'it's-not-my-job' group. They seem to devote more energy to getting out of work than actually doing it. Their favorite line is, 'That's not in my job description.' If you want to throw them a softball, you just say, 'Wow, it sounds like you're really busy.' They respond earnestly, 'You have no idea.' Their idea of thrill-seeking is to venture out to a new place for lunch."

"So there's the proof. You have a perfect case study."

"Izzy, what about the second test?"

Izzy paused and sifted through his infinite store of curious anecdotes.

"Marcus, I have a painting at home by Gillian Heath, the famous Chicago landscape artist."

"No kidding. I've seen some of her work. It's amazing."

"I can tell you it wasn't always amazing. The piece I have is terrible. In fact, it's hard to believe she painted it, but she did. You know how I know that?"

"Did she sign it?"

"She signed her name in the bottom, right-hand corner. In fact, I called her once just to make sure it was really her signature. I described the painting, and she laughed and said she should have let the painting remain anonymous. Do you know why I keep it? It's not because I like it. I don't like it. I keep it because she painted it, I like her work, and she's become a world-renowned artist. You would never know that if you saw the painting. Even when she was learning and stumbling, she signed her name. Her paintings weren't always great, but she still signed them. She claimed her work and her results.

"Marcus, the second test is the test of owning results. When you become a leader, you're responsible for the results of others as well as your own. Sometimes the results are good, sometimes they're bad. The test is to see if you will claim them when they're bad. What's the temptation?" asked Izzy.

"To blame somebody else."

"That's right. Point the finger, hide, cover up, create a diversion, make excuses—people do a lot of different things. But leaders are different. Leaders are like Gillian. They're willing to sign their names. When things don't go well, you know there's a leader in the house if there's a big signature, a big John Hancock somewhere, that tells you who is claiming the results. That's the second test: Sign your name."

The Second Test: Sign Your Name.

"Now comes the third test."

"I'm ready."

Marcus, you're a reasonably tolerable person to be around."

"Well, thanks Izzy."

"If you don't pass the third test, however, that could change. The third test adds more pressure to the relationship between stewardship and self-interest. Let me explain it this way. Did I ever tell you that I went to high school here too?"

"Only about a million times."

"Did you know that next week is my 30-year high school reunion?"

"Congratulations," replied Marcus.

"Thank you. It will be sharing time for some and show time for others. About half-way through the evening, Chester, one of our illustrious classmates will show up. He'll make his carefully choreographed appearance, as he always does, with a new trophy wife on his arm and a new hair piece on his head. He'll regale us with glorious triumphs about new ventures, asset values, and the heavy burdens of being a high-net-worth individual. After a few minutes, his charisma will overwhelm us and we'll have to leave to get a little oxygen. By the end of the night, he will once again announce his considered opinion that he should have been voted 'most likely to succeed.' At that point, we will all reflect with feelings of remorse, acknowledging the mistake and the irreversible suffering it has caused. He will then make his lonely exit, and we will not see our forlorn friend for another ten years."

Marcus collapsed with laughter.

"Ask yourself this question, Marcus. Are you comfortable making your primary contribution through other people? Remember, the transition to leading others is hard because the nature of contribution changes. Even if you become the CEO someday, the way you make your contribution won't change as dramatically as it will if you take this job.

"It requires a psychological adjustment. Fake leaders feel threatened by the success of others. Real leaders rejoice in the success of others. They find deep satisfaction in the triumphs of those they lead. If you can do this, you can lead. If you can't, leadership is not your game."

"Izzy, you know that I like to do things myself and I'm very competitive."

"That's breaking news," Izzy said teasingly. "Marcus, you've seen leaders who can't pass the third test. Their greatest fear is to be invisible, which they consider a fate worse than death. So they hoard recognition and steal credit. They just won't get off the stage.

"There will be times when things go well and there's plenty of recognition to go around. There will be other times when recognition has to be rationed. And finally, there will be times when there's no recognition at all. When there's plenty, serve yourself last. When it has to be rationed, don't take any. When there's none, make some and give it away. A leader is someone who enjoys recognition as much as the next person, but has the ability to go without when necessary. Can you do that?"

"Honestly, I've never had to."

"You'll get the chance. There are times when achieving success is a long, hard slog and there isn't recognition to go around. You have to feed yourself last or go without. This is one of the keys to engaging people and drawing out their discretionary efforts. You've got to be able to share the stage."

The Third Test: Share the Stage.

"I think I can do that—at least better than Chester."

"Are you ready for the fourth test?" asked Izzy.

"Absolutely."

"Marcus, I became a teacher 23 years ago. To qualify myself, I had to go to college and earn a degree. I had to acquire certain knowledge and skills so that I could teach. This is true for most any job. I have a friend in town who's a judge. She had to work hard for many years to qualify herself for that position.

"I went to work as a teacher. She went to work as a judge. But there was something curiously different about the two jobs. Her job came with an oath of office. Mine didn't. Before she could do her job, she had to raise her hand and swear that she would faithfully and impartially discharge and perform all of her duties under the law. In other words, she had to promise to act with honesty and integrity. Unfortunately, most jobs don't come with oaths. Did your job come with an oath?"

"Just an oath to work 24/7 and never go home," Marcus said with a chuckle.

"Isn't it interesting that only a few jobs carry oaths because society believes they hold the public trust. What about the rest of us? Don't we all hold the public trust? How about a teacher? How about a software developer? Goodness, the entire world runs on software. Who doesn't hold the public trust? Whose private decisions don't have public consequences?

"Marcus, most leaders start out honest. They want to do the right thing, but they get sucked into a vortex of compromise that can turn them into fake leaders. Even small acts of entitlement can suck you in."

Marcus started to laugh.

"What so funny?" asked Izzy.

"That reminds me of our last company dinner. Didn't I tell you about that?"

"No, I don't think so."

"This is a classic case of what you're talking about. It was our big company dinner last December. All 700 employees were there. We filled the entire hotel ballroom. You know, financially it was a tough year for the company. We barely broke even, so they downgraded the menu and served a measly piece of chicken. Everybody got the same thing. Well, apparently, our CEO wasn't aware that you could have anything on the menu as long as it was chicken. When they served him the entrée, he looked at it, scowled, and then motioned over the server. They had a word and the server left. About five minutes later the server came back, took the CEO's plate and replaced it with an enormous cut of prime rib!

"In front of everyone, he had the audacity to special order something else."

"Then what did he do?" Izzy asked.

"He just went on as if nothing happened. Got out his steak knife and dug right in. The story went viral the next day. They nicknamed him 'Mr. Prime Time.'"

"People may laugh at that and say it's not a big deal," said Izzy. "Certainly, it's not a terrible breach of ethics, but it is a tragic comedy. He traded his credibility for a piece of meat. Not a good exchange. The bigger concern is the dangerous thinking. He must have felt entitled to reward himself somehow—and in public no less.

"Marcus, let the rewards find you. Resist the temptation to reward yourself. It's easy to start small and convince yourself that you deserve something because you've delivered results, you've sacrificed and delayed gratification, and now it's your turn. It's at this point that the vortex of compromise can suck you all the way to ethical misconduct."

The teacher looked squarely at his student. "Marcus, what ethical standard do you want to live by?"

"The highest."

"Then take the oath. Bind yourself to act with honesty and integrity. That's the fourth test."

The Fourth Test: Take the Oath.

"It's a personal oath. You make it on your own. Society doesn't require it. The organization doesn't require it. You will quietly and privately hold yourself accountable to the public trust. The oath you make is enforceable only by you.

"Marcus, I'm old-fashioned on this issue. Shakespeare said, 'The purest treasure mortal times afford is spotless reputation.' That's what you have to gain. You're building a brand and it's all you've got. You have the opportunity to become a leader beyond reproach. Just watch. When things get tough, when people face uncertainty and potential loss, they will come to you. They will want a real leader, not a fake one.

"Marcus, if you take this job, there will be a series of ethical dilemmas along the way. Sometimes, there will be a lot at stake. You will have to choose between an unprincipled gain and a principled loss. An oath will give you the strength to walk away from an unprincipled gain and take a principled loss, if that's what it takes to do the right thing."

"Izzy, I'm facing one of those dilemmas right now."

"Tell me about it."

"My old boss had a company car that I get if I take the job."

"That sounds pretty good, Marcus."

"Except that he wasn't supposed to have the car. An executive he was close to broke the rules and got it for him under the table. He didn't actually meet the qualifications for a company car, and neither do I."

"Did you talk to the human resources department about it?"

"I did. The director told me to keep the car and not worry about it."

"And?"

Marcus responded mournfully, "They're going to give me the keys to a new car."

"What did I tell you, Marcus? The tests will come. I just didn't think they would come so soon. Without an oath, the analysis goes like this: Look at the potential for personal gain. Now look at the risk of personal loss. Compare the two. So in this case, the potential gain is high and the personal risk is low. You would keep the car."

The teacher reached over and put his hand on the student's knee. "Now let's add the oath to the equation. If a course of action is at odds with stewardship, you don't take it— regardless of what's at stake. If you do not stand on principle, you do not stand. There is nothing left to stand *on*. Without stewardship and the oath to bind you to it, leadership does not exist. You are reduced to a rational actor who spends his days in the pursuit of self-gratification. If you go through life this way, one day you will sit for your last portrait before they plant you, and your friends will try to think of some fitting tribute to your life. What will they say? Life was a carnival and he rode the rides? How very impressive that will be."

"I didn't like the car anyway," responded Marcus.

"I'm glad to hear that," said Izzy. "Are you ready to hear the final test?"

"I'm ready."

"Marcus, there's a get-rich theory of life that many people subscribe to. But there's another get-rich theory of life that has nothing to do with money? If you pass the fifth test, you'll be a rich man. As for money, I make no promises."

"Sounds interesting."

"Did I ever tell you about Mrs. Lee?"

"I don't think so."

"Mrs. Lee ran a deli around the corner from my house when I was growing up. My mother died when I was eight and my Dad worked a rotating Timken schedule at the steel mill, so I was on my own most of the time. As a teenager, I felt lost and got into a lot of trouble.

"One day I walked into Mrs. Lee's deli, took a sandwich, stuffed it in my coat, and walked out. I went back a few days later and Mrs. Lee motioned me over to the counter. She told me she had seen me take the sandwich. And then to my surprise, she asked me if I was hungry. I told her that I didn't have any money and that I was sorry for taking the sandwich. She said not to worry and made me a giant pastrami on rye.

"She put the sandwich on a plate, pushed it in front of me, and then asked me if I wanted to come to work for her in the Deli. I was 14 years old. At my high school graduation, my Dad was tapping the blast furnace on a swing shift, but Mrs. Lee was on the front row. For some reason, she took a special interest in me. I worked alongside this widowed woman for four years, making sandwiches, washing dishes, and stocking shelves.

"Every day after school I would go straight to the deli and put on my apron. Before she would let me start working, she would make me a sandwich and pour me something to drink. As the days, months, and years went by, she poured into me a sense of my own identity. From the small cup of her seemingly unremarkable life, she poured in love and confidence that never went away. Why did she care about me? I honestly didn't know. What I did know was that I didn't want to let her down. She told me that I wasn't dumb. I believed her. She told me that I mattered. I believed her. She told me that if I could influence a few lives for good, I would be a success. I believed her. I still believe her.

"Marcus, the fifth test is to pour your cup. Whatever your talents, whatever your capacity, pour your cup into the lives of others. The ironic thing about the fifth test is that if you pass all of the others, but fail this one, you will come up short.

"The great paradox of life is that pouring your cup fills it up. I'm not quite sure why it works this way, but it does. The more you pour, the more it's filled. This is the other get-rich theory of life. This is where you find your greatest joys and deepest satisfactions. But you can't take my word for it. You have to discover it for yourself.

"Write it down, Marcus. Pour your cup."

The Fifth Test: Pour Your Cup.

Marcus nodded in silent approval.

"Marcus, you are now in possession of the leadership test. Let's go over it one more time."

The Test

Putting stewardship above self-interest is an act of leadership. Throughout your life, you will be tested in five different ways to do this very thing.

1. **Fill Your Pack.**

2. **Sign Your Name.**

3. **Share the Stage.**

4. **Take the Oath.**

5. **Pour Your Cup.**

This was the test.

CHAPTER

6

The Grade

"Marcus."

"Izzy, did the computers arrive?"

"Two whole pallets! I took one out of the box. It's gorgeous. The school district's never had the money. You know the junk we've had. Finally, a real lab!"

"Excellent, excellent," exclaimed Marcus.

"Marcus, did I tell you? They're going to set it up in the next classroom."

"That's perfect. Then you can keep an eye on everything."

"Marcus, I can't thank you enough. I'm still in shock. How in the world did you do this? You didn't become the CEO and forget to tell me about it, did you?"

Marcus laughed. "I wish. You should know better than to ask me that. Influence and intent, Izzy, influence and intent!"

The teacher was bursting with pride.

"Izzy, do you remember the leadership test we talked about a few years back?"

"I was just thinking about what a struggle it was for you to take the job. Now what's it been, three years?"

"It's actually been four."

"Incredible."

"Izzy, I've passed four of the five tests so far."

"What about the fifth?"

"Almost."

"What do you mean, almost?"

"I haven't quite passed, but I'm close."

"When will you pass the fifth test?" asked Izzy.

"I'll have to hold you in suspense on that one—
to be continued as they say."

"Marcus, that's not fair."

"Oh, Izzy, it's eminently fair."

*****

Two weeks later the new semester began.
Before the morning bell, Izzy emerged from
his classroom to join the wave of chatter. He
was about to make his first eye contact and
trade his first affirmation when he noticed a
tall, smartly dressed gentleman approaching
him in the hall.

"Hello, Mr. Kroll," said the gentleman, with an out-stretched hand. "I'm the new computer science teacher. Perhaps we could have lunch sometime."

Marcus turned and walked into the classroom, leaving a bookish little man with an irrepressible smile.

Halfway through the class period, a knock came at the classroom door.

"Come in," said Marcus.

Izzy poked his head inside and made eye contact with his student for the last time.

"A-plus, my friend. A-plus."

This was the grade.

SELF-ASSESSMENT

Every leader has a stewardship. It may be big or small. That's not what matters. What matters is whether you can put stewardship above self-interest and consistently perform acts of leadership based on your influence and intent.

The following self-assessment will allow you to gain a sense of where you are today in terms of your current performance as a leader.

Using a 1-to-7 scale, where 1 means "Strongly Disagree" and 7 means "Strongly Agree," please rate yourself on each of the following five statements. The five statements correspond to the five tests of leadership.

THE LEADERSHIP TEST

1. I consistently demonstrate a pattern of <u>filling my pack</u> with responsibilities based on good judgment and a willingness to help.

Strongly Disagree						Strongly Agree
1	2	3	4	5	6	7

2. I consistently demonstrate a pattern of <u>signing my name</u> to the results of those I lead when they are poor results.

Strongly Disagree						Strongly Agree
1	2	3	4	5	6	7

3. I consistently demonstrate a pattern of <u>sharing the stage</u> with others by giving them recognition first and taking recognition for myself last.

Strongly Disagree						Strongly Agree
1	2	3	4	5	6	7

4. I consistently demonstrate a pattern of <u>taking the oath</u> by drawing a clear distinction between my stewardship and my self-interest, and by acting with honesty and integrity.

Strongly Disagree						Strongly Agree
1	2	3	4	5	6	7

5. I consistently demonstrate a pattern of <u>pouring my cup</u> into the lives of others by mentoring those who might benefit from my unique experience, talents, and abilities.

Strongly Disagree						Strongly Agree
1	2	3	4	5	6	7

Taking this assessment is an invitation to improve. Regardless of your starting point, you can become a better leader if you apply the simple truths that Izzy taught Marcus. Set specific goals for yourself and mark your progress along the way. Pass the test!

ACKNOWLEDGEMENTS

I wish to gratefully acknowledge several people who provided guidance and patient assistance with the different phases of this project.

I owe special thanks to those who offered advice and feedback on the project and manuscript. First in line is my wife, Tracey, who has poured her cup into my life. Others who have given indispensable help include Wesley Bull, Richard and Penny Clark, Jon Clark, Joel Clark, Tim Clark, Jr., Nick Fennell, Conrad Gottfredson, Brad Hokanson, Bryan Irving, Pete Rossi, Dane and Sherry Watkins, Dustin Willmore, and Christie Winterton.

My editors, Elizabeth Hokanson and Michael Lichfield, lent their invaluable expertise in helping prepare the manuscript for printing.

For her exceptional cover art and layout design, I wish to thank Kelli Nilson.

ABOUT THE AUTHOR

Timothy R. Clark is CEO of TRCLARK LLC, an international consulting and training organization that focuses on leadership, strategy, and change. A widely sought-after advisor and speaker, Dr. Clark works with leaders and organizations around the world. He has consulted with organizations such as Accenture, Accor, AmerisourceBergen, Chevron, CIGNA, Eli Lilly, Intel, Ketchum, Motorola, Northwestern Memorial Hospital, U.S. Department of Treasury, U.S. Department of Homeland Security, Wells Fargo & Company, and many others. An international expert in change leadership, Dr. Clark is the author of the landmark book, *Epic Change: How to Lead Change in the Global Age* (2008 Jossey-Bass).

Dr. Clark earned a doctorate from Oxford University and was a Fulbright and British Research Scholar. He also earned a master's degree from the University of Utah. As an undergraduate student, he completed a triple degree and was named a first-team Academic

All-American football player at Brigham Young University.

Before founding TRCLARK, Dr. Clark was the CEO of a mid-sized consulting firm based in Boston, Massachusetts. Prior to that assignment, he worked for Geneva Steel Company and was vice president of operations and plant manager for several years. Dr. Clark began his professional career at what is now Harris Interactive as a survey research project manager.

PERSONAL AND ORGANIZATIONAL SOLUTIONS

Book Orders

For regular book orders, bulk orders, or signed and personalized orders of *The Leadership Test*, please visit www.theleadershiptest.com, or call (801) 763-0640.

Speaking Engagements

If your organization would like to schedule Dr. Clark for a speaking engagement, please email at contactus@trclarkglobal.com or call (801) 763-0640.

Training and Coaching Solutions

TRCLARK offers customized instructor-led and web-based training and coaching solutions for organizations based on *The Leadership Test*. The solutions focus on helping leaders and organizations make a significant improvement in the quality and results of their leadership through the practical application of the concepts addressed in the book. If you would be interested in learning more about *The Leadership Test* training and coaching solutions, please email at contactus@trclarkglobal.com or call (801) 763-0640.

Visit: www.theleadershiptest.com

Visit: trclark.wordpress.com